My Emotions
Mes émotions

BORED
L'ENNUI

A Crabtree Roots Book
Un livre de la collection Les racines de Crabtree

AMY CULLIFORD

Crabtree Publishing
crabtreebooks.com

School-to-Home Support for Caregivers and Teachers

This book helps children grow by letting them practice reading. Here are a few guiding questions to help the reader with building his or her comprehension skills. Possible answers appear here in red.

Before Reading:

- What do I think this book is about?
    - *This book is about feeling bored.*
    - *This book is about what feeling bored looks or feels like.*
- What do I want to learn about this topic?
    - *I want to learn what makes people feel bored.*
    - *I want to learn what feeling bored looks like.*

During Reading:

- I wonder why...
    - *I wonder why we yawn when we are bored.*
    - *I wonder what we can do when we are bored.*

What have I learned so far?

- *I have learned that you can read if you are bored.*
- *I have learned that you can play a game if you are bored.*

After Reading:

- What details did I learn about this topic?
    - *I have learned that it is okay to feel bored.*
    - *I have learned that there are many things you can do when you feel bored.*
- Read the book again and look for the vocabulary words.
    - *I see the word **rains** on page 4 and the word **yawn** on page 6. The other vocabulary words are found on page 14.*

Soutien de l'école à la maison pour les parents, les gardiens et les enseignants

Ce livre aide les enfants à se développer grâce à la pratique de la lecture. Voici quelques exemples de questions pour aider le lecteur ou la lectrice à développer ses capacités de compréhension. Les suggestions de réponses sont indiquées en rouge.

Avant la lecture

- De quoi ce livre parle-t-il?
    - *Ce livre parle du sentiment de l'ennui.*
    - *Ce livre explique à quoi ressemble l'ennui ou ce que l'on ressent.*
- Qu'est-ce que je veux apprendre sur ce sujet?
    - *Je veux apprendre pourquoi les gens s'ennuient.*
    - *Je veux apprendre à quoi ressemble le sentiment de l'ennui.*

Pendant la lecture

- Je me demande pourquoi...
    - *Je me demande pourquoi je bâille quand je m'ennuie.*
    - *Je me demande ce que je peux faire quand je m'ennuie.*
- Qu'est-ce que j'ai appris jusqu'à présent?
    - *J'ai appris que je peux lire quand je m'ennuie.*
    - *J'ai appris que je peux jouer à un jeu quand je m'ennuie.*

Après la lecture

- Nomme quelques détails que tu as retenus.
    - *J'ai appris que c'est normal de **s'ennuyer**.*
    - *J'ai appris qu'il y a plusieurs choses à faire quand je m'ennuie.*
- Lis le livre à nouveau et cherche les mots de vocabulaire.
    - *Je vois le mot **pleut** à la page 4 et le mot **bâille** à la page 6. Les autres mots de vocabulaire se trouvent à la page 14.*

I am **bored**.

Je m'**ennuie**.

I am bored when it **rains**.

Je m'ennuie quand il **pleut**.

I **yawn** when I am bored.

Je **bâille** quand je m'ennuie.

I am bored in the **car**.

Je m'ennuie dans la **voiture**.

I **read** when I am bored.

Je **lis** quand je m'ennuie.

I play a **game** when I am bored.

Je joue à un **jeu** quand je m'ennuie.

When do you feel bored?

Quand t’ennuies-tu?

Word List

Sight Words

a
am
do
I
it
play
the
when
you

Liste de mots

Mots courants

je
joue
la
quand
tu
un

Words to Know
La boîte à mots

bored
ennuie

car
voiture

game
jeu

rains
pleut

read
lis

yawn
bâille

40 Words

I am **bored**.

I am bored when it **rains**.

I **yawn** when I am bored.

I am bored in the **car**.

I **read** when I am bored.

I play a **game** when I am bored.

When do you feel bored?

32 mots

Je m'**ennuie**.

Je m'ennuie quand il **pleut**.

Je **bâille** quand je m'ennuie.

Je m'ennuie dans la **voiture**.

Je **lis** quand je m'ennuie.

Je joue à un **jeu** quand je m'ennuie.

Quand t'ennuies-tu?

My Emotions

BORED

Mes émotions

L'ENNUI

Written by/Autrice: Amy Culliford
Designed by/Conception: Rhea Wallace
Series Development/Développement des séries: James Earley
Proofreader/Relectrice: Ellen Rodger
Educational Consultant/Conseillère pédagogique: Marie Lemke M.Ed.

Photographs/**photographies**:
Shutterstock: Juan Pablo Gonzaález: cover; diplomedia: p. 1; Syda Productions: p. 3, 14; GOLFX: p. 5, 14; airdone: p. 7, 14; Leszek Glasner: p. 8-9, 14; Zurijeta: p. 10, 14; Motortion Films: p. 11, 14; fizkes: p. 13

Crabtree Publishing

crabtreebooks.com 800-387-7650

Published in Canada
Publié au Canada
Crabtree Publishing
616 Welland Ave.
St. Catharines, Ontario
L2M 5V6

Published in the United Sta
Publié aux États-Unis
Crabtree Publishing
347 Fifth Avenue,
Suite 1402-145
New York, NY, 10016

Paperback	978-1-0398-5076-7
Ebook (pdf)	9781-0398-5118-4
Epub	9781-0398-5160-3

Printed in Canada/122023/CP20231116

Library and Archives Canada Cataloguing in Publication
Available at the Library and Archives Canada

Library of Congress Cataloging-in-Publication Data
Available at the Library of Congress